Lawyer, George Wythe.
Venerable Statesman, Jurist, and Educator

For Matt — another favorite!
From Card
April 7, 2013

George Wythe
Venerable Statesman, Jurist, and Educator

Copyright © 2007 Aleck Loker
All rights reserved

No part of this book shall be reproduced, stored in a retrieval system, or transmitted by any means without written permission from the author.

ISBN-10   1-928874-13-4
ISBN-13   978-1-928874-13-3

Printed in the United States of America

Published by:

Solitude Press
212 Brooks Street
Williamsburg VA 23185

An old man lay dying in his home on Shockoe Hill in Richmond. His body had been wracked by agonizing cramps for two weeks. It was an unjust end for a man known throughout the Commonwealth of Virginia, in fact known throughout the new nation, as a paragon of virtue, a model of ethical deportment among attorneys, a guiding influence through the American Revolution and the subsequent development of the United States government.

This pathetic scene came about from the basest of emotions—greed and ingratitude—in this case the emotions of the old man's namesake and great-nephew. The teenage boy badly abused the trust and affection of his great-uncle by poisoning his morning coffee the day after he learned from the old man's will that he was his principal heir but would have to share part of the estate with a young black man.

The grand old man brought to such an inglorious end was George Wythe: teacher, attorney, distinguished jurist, and mentor of many of Virginia's finest statesmen. His alleged murderer was George Wythe Sweeney, grandson of Wythe's sister. As we examine George Wythe's illustrious life, we'll learn how he impacted in a positive way so many Americans, making his untimely death all the more tragic.

Early Life

George Wythe was born in Elizabeth City County, Virginia in 1726 to Thomas Wythe III and his wife Margaret Walker Wythe. Thomas III died three years later, a relatively young man about thirty-four-years old. Thomas I, and Thomas II, George's grandfather and great-grandfather, also died young. The Wythes came to Virginia from Norfolk, England about 1680. Thomas Wythe I, Gentleman, achieved some prominence in Elizabeth City County, serving as justice of the peace and member of the House of Burgesses. Thomas II also served as justice of the peace and as a trustee of the town of Hampton, but survived his father by only four months. Thomas III continued the tradition by representing Elizabeth City County in the House of Burgesses, served as a local magistrate, and added to the wealth accumulated by the two previous generations. He was a planter and half-owner of a wharf in Hampton, the principal port in Virginia at that time. He lived at *Chesterville,* an estate that is now part of the Langley Research Center in Hampton. Elizabeth City County has been absorbed by the City of Hampton.

Thomas and Margaret Wythe had three children: Thomas IV, Anne, and George. When George's father died, the bulk of his estate passed to George's elder brother. George received several slaves and some personal effects as his inheritance. He was an infant at that time. Margaret Wythe chose to educate George at home rather than send him to the Syms Free School nearby. Margaret, daughter of a prominent Hampton Quaker, had been well educated, and she taught George Latin and Greek as well as mathematics, logic, and grammar. She instilled in her young son a Quaker respect for all mankind, a love for the classics, for logic, and science that would distinguish him throughout his long life. He must have inherited from his mother a strong constitution because he greatly exceeded the lives of his paternal ancestors and could have lived much longer had not a murderer ended his life.

When George Wythe turned fourteen, he attended the grammar school at William and Mary. Two years later, he chose a career: attorney. He had two likely paths to pursue in following such a career. He could go to London and study at one of the Inns of Court, or he could remain in America and read law as an apprentice to a licensed attorney. George chose the latter path. His uncle, Stephen Dewey, who was married to Margaret Wythe's sister, had his law office in Charles City County. George went there and began his studies. He spent two years under his uncle's tutelage and then returned to *Chesterville* where he continued his studies on his own. While there, his mother died.

When he felt he had sufficiently prepared, George rode to Williamsburg and presented himself for the examination and admittance to the bar. His examiners were Peyton Randolph, Saint Lawrence Burford, William Nimmo, and George's uncle Stephen Dewey. George Wythe passed easily and received his license to practice law on June 18, 1746. He was twenty.

Since his brother was settled at *Chesterville,* George moved to Spotsylvania County where he could begin his law practice and live independently. He received his license to practice law in Spotsylvania County in November, 1746. George lived with Zachary Lewis, the King's Attorney in that county. Lewis needed someone to help with his case load and George came highly recommended. Soon George took an interest in Zachary Lewis' daughter, Ann. Their marriage license was issued on December 26, 1747. The Lewis family had clearly welcomed George Wythe into their hearts, and he must have looked forward to many pleasant and rewarding years among them.

But in little more than seven months, Ann had contracted a fever and died. George Wythe was bereft at her loss. He later wrote that he drowned his sorrow in the inns of Spotsylvania County. If so, he soon put that behind him because he had relocated to Williamsburg by October 1748—three months after his wife's death. He joined Ann's uncle, Benjamin Waller, in his law practice in Williamsburg and the surrounding counties.

A Fresh Start

At that time, Williamsburg was a thriving, if small, town of 1,000 to 2,000 residents. When the General Assembly convened in April and October, the town population more than doubled, with visitors attending the legislative sessions and participating in the horse races and auctions that occurred at the same time. Wythe saw that a law practice in the capital city of the Virginia colony would afford him more opportunities; it was a place where he could make a fresh start. The proximity of the College of William and Mary was also no doubt attractive to Wythe, whose keen interest in the classics, philosophy, and science remained as strong as ever. Here he could enjoy the stimulating company of like-minded academics.

Reconstructed Colonial Williamsburg Capitol of 1705

The government of Virginia at that time was vested in a resident governor who received instructions from the Privy Council and the Board of Trade in London. The power of the governor extended to the right to appoint all but the lowest public officials and militia officers. He received advice from a council composed of twelve members appointed by the crown for life. Those council members invariably came from the loyal landed gentry that took the place of nobility in the colony.

The governor had veto power over legislation passed by the General Assembly composed of the House of Burgesses and the Council. And he could prorogue or dissolve the General Assembly whenever he felt they had overstepped their bounds.

Besides embarking on his law career, on October 28, 1748, George Wythe was selected to serve as the clerk of two important standing committees in the House of Burgesses: the Privileges and Elections Committee, and the Propositions and Grievances Committee. This was his first step in a long political career. He was probably helped along by Benjamin Waller and by the contacts Wythe had already made in the House of Burgesses, including his uncle, and men such as Peyton Randolph, who had examined his mastery of the law just two years before. His duties as clerk consisted of taking and presenting the minutes of the committee meetings.

George Wythe, as a young and unproven attorney in Williamsburg, would have had stiff competition from men such as John and Peyton Randolph, Robert Carter Nicholas, and later Edmund Pendleton. However, within a few years, George Wythe had secured some very important clients including John Blair, an attorney himself and great-nephew of Reverend James Blair (the founder and first president of the College of William and Mary), Henry Fitzhugh of King George County, and the prominent Custis family of New Kent County. (Martha Dandridge Custis, widow, would marry Wythe's good friend George Washington in 1759.)

Wythe added Robert Carter to his distinguished list of wealthy clients within a few years.

Wythe brought a strict sense of integrity to the practice of law. He insisted that his clients tell him the truth. If he found that they failed to do so, he would return their fees and refuse to represent them. In a profession not always noted for taking the high moral ground, George Wythe behaved in a way that was beyond reproach. His adherence to the strictest ethical standard added to his reputation and eventually led him to an outstanding career as a jurist and a law professor. Reverend Lee Massey went so far as to call George Wythe "the only honest lawyer I ever knew."

Beginning of a Political Career

Resident Governor Robert Dinwiddie had received permission from the London-based Board of Trade to charge a fee for applying his signature to land grants in Virginia. Virginia had been without a resident governor for a couple of years and, by 1751, Dinwiddie knew that a large backlog of land grants awaited his signature to make them legal. He was authorized to charge one pistole (nearly £1 then, about $240 today) as his fee for signing each land grant, the customary fee in other colonies but unheard of in Virginia. The House of Burgesses protested that the governor had not consulted with them or the Council about this fee and felt it should not be applied. In 1752, the House passed a resolution stating, "Whoever shall here-after pay pistole, as a Fee to the Governor, for Use of the Seal to Patents for Lands, shall be deemed a

Betrayer of the Rights and Privileges of the People." The House dispatched Peyton Randolph, who served as the King's Attorney, to London to argue against Governor Dinwiddie's fee. Randolph sailed in December 1753, without the governor's permission.

Angered, Dinwiddie accused Randolph of abandoning his post and appointed George Wythe in January 1754 to serve as the King's Attorney—a rapid rise for this young attorney plucked from the midst of so many renowned lawyers in Williamsburg. George Wythe held the legal opinion that the governor had the right to charge the fee for endorsing the land grants—an unpopular opinion, but one that Wythe felt was legally correct. Wythe's appointment to Randolph's position, however, put him in an awkward situation as a usurper of one of the most popular men in the colony.

Later in August, 1754, when Williamsburg's legislative representative Armistead Burwell died, the House of Burgesses selected George Wythe to fill the vacancy. This began Wythe's long career as a member of the legislature. Wythe assured the members of the House that he would resign his post as King's Attorney as soon as Randolph returned from England.

Wythe soon found himself embroiled in another political tussle. This occurred when the House of Burgesses appropriated £20,000 to support Colonel George Washington's campaign in the French and Indian War. In doing so, they stipulated that the expenditures would be subject to the oversight of a House committee. Governor Robert Dinwiddie, who had already dispatched Washington to the Ohio Valley to oppose the French there, felt the House of Burgesses had no right to review how he spent appropriated funds. He bristled at their impertinence. His friend George Wythe was appointed to the committee of oversight. Throughout his life, Wythe would occupy such difficult positions and prove himself able to broker reasonable compromises.

Colonial Williamsburg Courthouse

Peyton Randolph returned from England in 1755, having received an agreement that the governor's authority regarding taxation would be limited and that Randolph could resume his duties as King's Attorney. That same year Thomas Wythe

IV died and George inherited not only the estate of *Chesterville* but also his brother's position on the Elizabeth City County court—a position traditionally held by the Wythes.

Wythe's fortunes were now accumulating, and as an eligible widower, he courted the young daughter of a prominent Williamsburg man, Richard Taliaferro. George's medium build, blue eyes, high forehead and arched brows, along with his solemn and serious demeanor, must have impressed Taliaferro's daughter. Elizabeth Taliaferro lived at the family plantation, *Powhatan,* about five miles outside the city in James City County. She and George were married in 1755. Richard Taliaferro, a wealthy landowner and architect, designed and built a small estate for his daughter and new son-in-law in the city. The handsome brick house, prominently placed between Bruton Parish Church and the Governor's Palace, would serve as the Wythe home for more than thirty years.

With Wythe's new duties as husband, busy attorney, and master of *Chesterville*, he neglected campaigning and failed to win election to the House of Burgesses from Elizabeth City County in 1756 and again in 1758. However, in 1758 he was chosen by the faculty of the College of William and Mary to represent the college in the House—a position formerly held by Peyton Randolph who had won election as a Williamsburg Burgess. Wythe served as the representative of the College of William and Mary in the House of Burgesses until 1761, when he successfully ran in the election for Elizabeth City County.

From Prominent Citizen of Williamsburg to Rebel

In 1758, Governor Francis Fauquier replaced Governor Dinwiddie. Fauquier was an intellectual with a broad range of interests including science (a member of the Royal Society), music, classical literature, philosophy, gambling and fine dining. He and his neighbor, George Wythe, soon forged a strong bond. They formed a small social circle that included Professor William Small from the College of William and Mary. Small, the only layman on the college faculty at that time, was professor of natural philosophy (science). Beginning in 1760, Thomas Jefferson, a young student at the college, became a regular participant in the dinners and discussions held by Wythe, the governor and Professor Small.

During this time, George Wythe established himself as one of the leading figures in the city of Williamsburg as well as the House of Burgesses. Wythe's powers of persuasion and negotiation frequently came into play as he took House bills to the Council for their consideration and concurrence.

One bill Wythe didn't support was the so-called Two Penny Act that temporarily limited the compensation for Anglican ministers in Virginia. Anglican ministers were due an annual payment of 16,000 pounds of tobacco. The crop shortage at that time inflated the value to about six pennies per pound. The Virginia General Assembly was considering legislation limiting the ministers' payments to one-third of the current price of tobacco.

Although Wythe opposed the bill—he represented the faculty of the College of William and Mary at the time, nearly all of whom were ordained clergy—but he failed to influence his fellow burgesses or the governor. When the Two Penny Act was signed into law, Reverend John Camm took the clergy's case before the Board of Trade in London and they found in favor of the ministers. On August 10, 1759, the king disallowed the Two Penny Act and reprimanded Fauquier for signing it. Camm was back in Virginia in 1760 with the official decree. This precipitated a number of law suits in the county courts brought by the Anglican clergy to have their full annual stipends restored.

In Elizabeth City County in 1763, George Wythe sat as the judge in the case brought by Reverend Thomas Warrington. Wythe guided the jury through the legal arguments and to their conclusion, which was in favor of the minister. However, Wythe overruled the jury. This at first seems surprising since he had opposed the Two Penny Act and had argued in favor of the clergy receiving their full compensation when the act was before the House of Burgesses. However, his response to the jury in this case illustrates an important facet of George Wythe's character: he would invariably come down on the side of the law as he interpreted it. In this case, he felt that the General Assembly had acted within their purview and the governor had signed the Two Penny Act into law in keeping with the English constitution as Wythe understood it. Therefore, he saw the Two Penny Act as the law of Virginia and argued that the crown had no business meddling in Virginia's local laws. Wythe's position coincided with Patrick Henry's position with regard to the Two Penny Act, although they arrived at their positions from markedly different perspectives. Wythe reached his conclusion from a logical and dispassionate analysis of the law as he saw it. Henry arrived at his position from his innate and passionate belief in the rights of citizens to govern their own affairs. It is noteworthy that Wythe took this position in opposition to the king thirteen years before the Declaration of Independence.

A year later, Wythe, as a member of the Committee of Correspondence, reviewed a letter from Edward Montague, Virginia's agent in London. Montague had forwarded the introduction of the infamous Stamp Act in Parliament.

The members of the committee were: John Blair, President of the Governor's Council; William Nelson, council member; Thomas Nelson, Secretary of State; Robert Carter, council member; John Robinson, Speaker of the House; Peyton Randolph, King's Attorney; Robert Carter Nicholas, member of the House of Burgesses; Lewis Burwell, member of the House of Burgesses; and George Wythe. After reviewing the letter from Montague and deliberation, the committee drafted the following resolution

Ordered that Mr. Montague be informed that this Colony is much alarmed at the attempt

in Parliament to lay a duty on the sev[eral] *commodities men*[tioned] *in their Votes, a copy of which he sent to ye com*[mittee] *particularly on Madeira wine & the proposal for a stamp duty. That he is desired to oppose this with all his influence & as far as he may venture to insist on the* **injustice of laying any duties on us & particularly taxing the internal trade of the colonies, without their consent***.*

Thus began the argument against "taxation without representation." George Wythe and Robert Carter Nicholas drafted the letter to Edward Montague on July 28, 1764. The Stamp Act issue was presented to the House of Burgesses in November of that year. The Committee of Correspondence proposed four resolutions calling for the drafting of an appeal directly to the king; a memo to the House of Lords requesting reconsideration; an admonition to the House of Commons; and a letter to the Massachusetts House of Representatives indicating their accord with that body over their opposition to the Stamp Act. Wythe composed the letter of admonition to the House of Commons. His letter was so strident that many members of the House of Burgesses could not accept it. He was clearly not among the most conservative or conciliatory members of the House.

His letter read in part:

They [the Council and the Burgesses] *conceive it is essential to British liberty, the laws imposing taxes on people, ought not to be made without the consent of representatives chosen by themselves, who, at the same time that they are acquainted with the circumstances of their constituents, sustain a portion of the burden laid on them.*

Wythe's letter, with alterations to make it acceptable to the House of Burgesses, made its way to London, but the House of Commons refused to have it entered into their deliberations. They passed the Stamp Act on March 8, 1765. Wythe and the other members of the General Assembly learned of the Common's action in May. A large number of the assembly left Williamsburg at that time, willing to wait and see what came next from Parliament.

On May 30, 1765, only 39 of the 116 burgesses remained in town. Patrick Henry, a new member from Louisa County, proposed five incendiary resolutions denouncing the Stamp Act. Although his resolutions were similar to the correspondence sent to London only months before, Richard Bland, Peyton Randolph and George Wythe opposed Henry. Their reason for doing so was that the resolutions added nothing new, and they felt that the points had been expressed in a more conciliatory tone in the previous correspondence to Parliament and the king. They argued that the previous correspondence had not yet been answered directly. They felt the House should wait a bit longer. Of course, they may also have been put off by the demeanor of the brash young man from Louisa County.

In spite of Wythe's and others' opposition, Patrick Henry's resolutions were passed and quickly appeared in the newspapers. Wythe and others moved to have the resolutions expunged from the record of the House of Burgesses, but the effort failed. Wythe clearly had not abandoned hope that the power of persuasion could be successful in the colonial dispute with the British king and Parliament. He didn't disagree with Patrick Henry in principle but only in the method to redress the unconstitutional position that they both believed Parliament had taken with the Stamp Act. Governor Fauquier quickly dissolved the General Assembly, viewing their resolutions as insubordinate.

George Wythe's Home in Williamsburg on the Palace Green

Wythe still enjoyed the admiration of Governor Fauquier, and when Speaker Robinson died, Peyton Randolph resigned as King's Attorney so that he could become Speaker of the House of Burgesses. Fauquier nominated his friend George Wythe to the King's Attorney position. Wythe wrote to Benjamin Franklin in London to have him lobby on behalf of his appointment to King's Attorney.

However, Wythe's efforts were unsuccessful. John Randolph, Peyton's brother, was made King's Attorney. John Randolph's loyalty to the crown had won him the plum position.

In 1768, George Wythe became mayor of the City of Williamsburg, an indication of his growing stature and popularity within the town. Also that year, Governor Fauquier died—a loss that George Wythe felt more than most Virginians. Fauquier had generally taken the side of the Virginians, to the extent that he could, in their disagreements with Parliament. His replacement, Norborne Berkeley, who had the title Lord Botetourt, would prove to be popular, but within two years he died. Botetourt was followed by a stern opponent of the colonial citizens, John Murray, the Earl of Dunmore, who would remain as governor until the outbreak of the American Revolution. Wythe clashed with Lord Dunmore early in his tenure when, sitting as the judge of the General Court, the governor refused to delay a case in which George Wythe and Robert Carter Nicholas were to be opposed by Edmund Pendleton and his missing associate. Lord Dunmore said, "Go on, Mr. Pendleton. You'll be a match for both of them." Wythe angrily replied, "With your Lordship's assistance!" Dunmore turned red and glared at Wythe. Wythe never enjoyed the close relationship with Lord Dunmore that he had experienced with governors Fauquier and Botetourt.

Wythe was now clearly on a collision course with those who would attempt to maintain London's control of the colonies. He had always been a strict adherent to the law and a well-read student of not only English common law but also classical democracy. He had taken his argument about self-governance from the philosophy of John Locke. He would find, as the next few years played out, that he could no longer support the king and Parliament.

Wythe's Role in the Revolution

During the period starting with the Townsend Act of 1767 up to the blockade of Boston Harbor in 1774, Wythe held the opinion that Parliament had no legal right to meddle with colonial internal trade or internal government within the colonies. He believed Virginia (and by extension, each of the other colonies) should be treated as an independent government giving allegiance to England's king or queen. Wythe had become one of the radicals who believed in the colonies' rights to self-governance. By 1774, Wythe held a position on the Williamsburg Committee of Safety along with Peyton Randolph, Robert Carter Nicholas and Benjamin Waller. That committee would wield executive authority over Virginia during the Revolution.

Wythe was as outraged as the rest of the public when he learned that Lord Dunmore had secretly seized the arms and powder from the magazine in Williamsburg. He exchanged his well-tailored but somber frock coat for a rough hunting shirt, grabbed a musket and marched in the military parade through the city. By June, 1775, Dunmore had fled the city and boarded HMS Fowey, never to return to his seat as governor. Wythe, accompanied by Elizabeth, traveled to Philadelphia for the Continental Congress in August 1775. Their route took them across the York River on Gooch's Ferry through Hobb's Hole (Tappahannock) and Port Royal, then by ferry across the Rappahannock and Potomac Rivers, through Baltimore, Wilmington and Chester. Philadelphia was the largest of the colonial cities at that time, with about 30,000 residents.

Wythe's friend Peyton Randolph chaired the Continental Congress. King George III had declared the colonies in a state of rebellion, and Wythe, as well as all the other delegates, was considered a ringleader in the rebellion. But there were moderates as well as radicals within the Congress. Wythe's stand became clear as he argued for establishment of free trade among the colonies. He said, "Turn your eyes to Concord, Lexington, Charleston, Bristol, New York. There you see the character of Ministry and Parliament." Those cities, of course, had already experienced violence and repression by British troops dispatched to restore compliance within the colonies. Wythe had concluded that the colonies needed to establish sources for goods independent of England and, to protect their rights to trade outside of England, they needed a navy.

While George and Elizabeth Wythe were in Philadelphia, their friend John Randolph had taken his family to England demonstrating his opposition to the stand taken by his brother Peyton and all the others among the Virginia delegation at the Congress. Peyton Randolph died in October of 1775 while still in Philadelphia.

During the winter of 1775-1776, Wythe continued as a member of the Congress. Elizabeth was back in Williamsburg. Wythe continued to press for the establishment of treaties with other nations. He asked the other delegates, "In what character shall we treat? As subjects of Great Britain? As rebels? Why should we be so fond of calling ourselves dutiful subjects? We must declare ourselves a free people." He called George III the "author of our miseries." By this time there could be no doubt that Wythe had abandoned any hope of changing Parliament's approach to the colonies through petition or conciliation. He recognized that the colonies would have to declare their independence from the mother country.

On June 7, 1776, Richard Henry Lee from Virginia offered a motion that the colonies formally declare their independence from Great Britain. John Adams of Massachusetts seconded the motion. But the question was postponed until July 1st to allow the delegations an opportunity to get the concurrence of their respective assemblies. Meanwhile, Wythe's protégé, Thomas Jefferson, was selected to draft the declaration. Lee and Wythe left Philadelphia to return to Williamsburg. Wythe had in his possession Thomas Jefferson's plan for the government of Virginia as a free and independent state.

When Wythe attended the Virginia Convention and offered Jefferson's plan for the delegates' consideration, they found it too liberal. Among some of the more controversial aspects were Jefferson's language providing for separation from the Church of England, manumission of the slaves, free education for all, and broader voting rights.

By the time Wythe returned to Philadelphia, the Declaration of Independence, written by Thomas Jefferson, with amendments by Franklin and Adams, had been signed by most of the delegates to the Continental Congress. Wythe added his signature in September, 1776, writing it above the names of the other Virginia delegates. By doing so he left no doubt that he wanted to be seen as a leader in the movement to separate from Great Britain.

One of his final accomplishments that session was to move the Continental Congress to appoint Thomas Jefferson, Benjamin Franklin and Silas Deane as the colonial agents in France—the first ambassadors of what would become the United States of America. However, Thomas Jefferson and his wife had moved in with Elizabeth Wythe in Williamsburg. Jefferson stayed in Virginia rather than traveling to France due to his wife's ill health. His interest in crafting the new Virginia government also may have influenced his decision. Jefferson pushed a bill through the Virginia Assembly to amend the new commonwealth constitution. With George Wythe's return, Jefferson saw to it that

Wythe would participate in re-drafting the Virginia laws along with Edmund Pendleton, George Mason, Thomas Ludwell Lee, and himself.

By March of 1777, Thomas Ludwell Lee had died; and Pendleton had fallen from his horse, his injuries preventing his attendance in committee. George Mason, tired of the tedious process, deferred to Jefferson and Wythe, who now had a free hand to finish the amendments to the Virginia Constitution as they saw fit. Soon, George Wythe was elected Speaker of the Virginia House of Delegates and assisted Governor Patrick Henry in ensuring that Virginia met its obligations to the Continental Army's war effort. During his tenure, he also saw the changes to the Virginia Constitution passed in the General Assembly. One notable provision of the new constitution created the Chancery Court and the General Court system. George Wythe and Robert Carter Nicholas became the Chancery Court Justices. The Chancery Court at that time was the highest level court in the commonwealth.

During the war, while the government moved to Richmond in 1780, Wythe maintained his home in Williamsburg. He remained there due to his loyalty to the college and the city, even though he was more exposed to possible capture there. Had he been captured by the British, he could have been returned to London for trial as a traitor. If found guilty, he would have been hanged, drawn and quartered. In June, 1781, General Charles Cornwallis came to Williamsburg and found the college closed due to a lack of students—they had enlisted in the Continental Army in time for the final battle at Yorktown.

It isn't clear where George and Elizabeth Wythe were when Cornwallis came to the city, but one apocryphal story tells that Wythe and some companions were hunting at the mouth of College Creek when they came upon an advance party of British marines attempting to land there. Supposedly Wythe and his friends opened fire on the British with their muskets loaded with bird shot. The British returned to their ship. About the same time, George Washington stayed in the city with George and Elizabeth Wythe prior to marching to his headquarters at Yorktown and his ultimate defeat of Cornwallis' forces.

Following the war, Wythe devoted much of his time to the process of converting a confederation of independent states into the new union of states as one nation under a strong federal government. Wythe took the side of the Federalists in his concept of how the United States of America should function. He went to Philadelphia to assist James Madison at the Federal Convention, but had to return to Williamsburg before any real progress had been made. Although only 48-years old, Elizabeth Wythe was critically ill. George Wythe sent his resignation to Philadelphia and remained by his wife's side. She died August 18, 1787.

Wythe represented Williamsburg in the subsequent Virginia Convention to ratify the new U. S. Constitution. In the summer of 1788, he served as Chairman of the Committee of the Whole, guiding discussion and debate by all the members of the convention. His legal rival, Edmund Pendleton, served as President of the Convention. Wythe and Pendleton ensured that the strong opposition by Patrick Henry and George Mason did not derail Virginia's ratification of the constitution. Wythe used his skills to develop a compromise that broke the opposition's resolve: Virginia would approve the constitution, recognizing that it had significant faults, and would draft proposed amendments for consideration in the new U. S. Congress to rectify those faults. The compromise worked and the proposed amendments are substantially reflected in the U. S. Bill of Rights ultimately adopted by Congress in New York in 1789 and finally ratified by the states in 1791.

Educator
  During the years leading up to the revolution, George Wythe worked as a plantation owner, a politician, and an attorney, activities which added to his growing wealth; but the activity that surely gave him the greatest sense of accomplishment was his role as a teacher. In 1760, Thomas Jefferson had come to Williamsburg, a seventeen-year-old student at the College of William and Mary. Soon, Jefferson became a private student living with and studying under George Wythe. During this arrangement, which lasted for about five years, the two men formed a lifelong bond of affection and mutual respect.
  Wythe taught Jefferson to love the classics in Latin and Greek, tutored him in the law, history, science, and mathematics. But Jefferson also

emulated other personal habits and beliefs of George Wythe. Wythe ate sparingly, eventually adopting a nearly exclusive vegetarian diet, and drank wine moderately. He took a cold shower bath every morning, even in winter, and adhered to a rigid schedule of work and studies. Wythe's Quaker background influenced him in his belief of fair treatment for Indians and African slaves. In their beliefs concerning slavery, he and Jefferson were both conflicted. They personally abhorred the practice of slavery but could not conceive of a successful strategy to abolish it completely. Wythe and Jefferson also shared a lifelong interest in applied science. They both believed in religious liberty, freedom of speech, and government by the consent of the governed.

Jefferson's time under Wythe's wing exposed him to a number of contrasts that helped him develop his character: abstemious Wythe versus gourmand Governor Fauquier; Wythe's measured and, at times, tedious lecturing in court or the legislature versus Patrick Henry's fiery and sometimes overwrought oratory; Wythe's conservative but carefully tailored clothing versus the flamboyant manner of dress of many of his contemporaries. During his studies with Wythe, Jefferson certainly observed how highly regarded Wythe was for his strict code of ethics and his insistence on adherence to the fundamental rights of the citizenry.

Wythe sought truth and logic in the world around him. He applied those tests in the practice of law, in his participation in the government, and in his relationships with others. Jefferson shared and, perhaps, adopted those traits from his mentor. At times, Wythe could seem aloof and dispassionate, particularly when compared to more flamboyant figures such as Patrick Henry. But he could also display a temper, particularly when nettled in the courtroom by his frequently successful opponent, Edmund Pendleton.

Wythe would take in other students, such as St. George Tucker in Williamsburg, and later, young Henry Clay in Richmond. Clay eventually went on to become the highly successful Kentucky representative in Congress, founder of the Whig party and, a man noted for his ability to broker a successful compromise, earning him the epithet "The Great Compromiser." He learned the power of compromise from his mentor, George Wythe.

The Wren Building, first academic structure at the College of William and Mary in Virginia

When Thomas Jefferson succeeded Patrick Henry as governor in 1779, he, along with James Madison, President of the College of William and Mary, introduced a number of reforms in the college. One in particular, the creation of a new Chair of Law and Police, established the first college law curriculum in America. Not surprisingly, they appointed George Wythe to be the first Professor of Law and Police at the College of William and Mary. There were eighty students at the college that year. They paid 1,000 pounds of tobacco as their fee and could attend lectures by two professors of their choosing.

Wythe's salary as a professor at the College of William and Mary was eight hogsheads (about 8,000 pounds) of tobacco. He set about creating a course of law studies that was unique, and features of his method of teaching continue to this day in law schools throughout the country. Wythe held classes in the Wren building and moot courts in the old Capitol building in Williamsburg. He also had his students participate in mock legislative sessions to gain experience in parliamentary procedures as well as debate. He stated that his goal was "to form such characters as may be fit to succeed those which have been ornamental and useful in the national councils of America." In other words he planned to train future statesmen of America. His law curriculum at the College of William and Mary clearly accomplished that goal. Future Chief Justice of the U. S. Supreme Court John Marshall, twenty-seven years old and fresh from the Continental

Army, studied law under George Wythe for about six weeks—the only formal legal training Marshall ever received.

Jurist

When the constitution of the Commonwealth of Virginia was amended in 1777, the highest court was designated as the Chancery Court. George Wythe was appointed as justice of the Chancery Court. Wythe served in that capacity until 1788. In one landmark case argued before Wythe's court by Edmund Pendleton, Wythe saw the key issue as one of whether the General Assembly could pardon prisoners in a treason case. Pendleton argued for the execution of the prisoners because the legislature had split on whether or not to grant them pardons. Wythe ruled that the constitution gave the power of pardon to the governor and the legislature had overstepped its bounds in voting on granting pardons. In his summation of the issues in the case, he invoked the principle of judicial review; Wythe said, "Nay more, if the whole legislature, an event to be deprecated, should attempt to over-leap the bounds, prescribed to them by the people, I, in administering the public justice of the country, will meet the united powers, at my seat in this tribunal; and pointing to the constitution, will say to them here is the limit of your authority; and hither shall you go, but no further."

In 1788, the Virginia legislature created a Court of Appeals consisting of five justices. This body became the highest level court in the commonwealth, putting it in a position to review decisions by the Chancery Court. Wythe chose to remain as the sole judge in the Court of Chancery in 1789, taking the title Chancellor of Virginia. His old rival, Edmund Pendleton received an appointment to the new Court of Appeals. This would result in no end of anguish for Wythe as he saw over the next six years 150 chancery cases appealed to the new Court of Appeals. A number of Wythe's decisions were overturned by Pendleton and the Court of Appeals much to Wythe's irritation. Indeed, he became so incensed that he wrote and paid for the publication of a book in 1795 taking issue with the Appeals Court rulings.

One case, at least, must have given him satisfaction. In *Page v. Pendleton & Lyons*, Wythe upheld in 1793 the proposition that Virginians must pay, in full, debts owed British creditors before the war. Wythe received considerable criticism from those who wanted to avoid paying debts they had incurred with British firms. But he considered that common law and decency mandated that the people should pay their just debts. Pendleton and Lyons had argued that the debts were no longer valid. The new Court of Appeals overturned the Chancery Court decision much to Pendleton's glee. But In 1796, the U. S. Supreme Court ruled that Wythe's decision was correct.

Wythe was a dedicated jurist who would serve as Chancellor for ten years—his career ended by death, not disfavor. One of his last cases allowed him to express his true feelings about slavery. (He had freed his own slaves at *Chesterville* and in Williamsburg.) In *Hudgins v. Wright*, Hudgins intended to send descendents of an Indian out of Virginia. The descendents argued that they were not slaves, but entitled to freedom based on their Indian ancestry. In his opinion in 1806, Wythe wrote, "freedom is the birthright of every human being…" His opinion came well ahead of its time.

Leaving Williamsburg

Once the Virginia government moved to Richmond, Williamsburg became less exciting for George Wythe. By 1789, he had reached an impasse with the administration of the College of William and Mary, and on September 15th, he resigned his professorship at the college. The cause of the dispute is unknown, but he continued to take young men into his home as private students.

In his Williamsburg home, his household consisted of Wythe, one or more students, his housekeeper, Lydia Broadnax, who had been his slave before he freed her, and several other servants. Wythe taught his students Greek, Latin, French, Spanish, English Literature and Arithmetic. One of his students at that time, Littleton Waller Tazewell, twelve years old, lived with Wythe since his father had moved the rest of the family to his estate called *Kingsmill*. Young Tazewell would grow up to be a distinguished U. S. Senator and Virginia Governor, another example of Wythe achieving his goal of preparing young men for statesmanship.

When Wythe resigned from the college, he took in a young man named William Munford who could not afford to pay tuition. Wythe taught him in his home for free. He even acquired scientific equipment to teach Munford physics. Munford would later write about this time in Wythe's life. His mentor had become more introverted after his wife's death and his resignation from the college. He would walk down the Duke of Gloucester Street in Williamsburg and not notice people or speak to them when they spoke to him. Wythe had always been aloof, but he had also always been cordial to the people around him. Townspeople could tell that something was bothering Chancellor Wythe. However, his physical health must have been fine. Munford wrote of one incident in which he and Wythe walked five miles from his house in the city to visit the Taliaferros at *Powhatan*. Wythe was deep in thought and unresponsive to Munford's conversation, but clearly he was in good physical condition if he was able to walk that distance at age sixty-six.

By 1791, Wythe decided to leave Williamsburg and move to Richmond. He missed the bustle of government activity; and the long journey to the new capital four times a year to attend to the Chancery Court duties had become a nuisance. There was little left in Williamsburg to hold him. He had lost his wife; he no longer had an association with the college, and the important affairs of government were no longer there. But Wythe would not abandon William Munford; he invited the young man to come to Richmond and continue to live as his guest and student. Lydia and the other household staff packed Wythe's belongings, including his treasured books and scientific equipment, loaded them into his coach and wagons, and made the long trip to Richmond in September, 1791 with Wythe and Munford.

Lydia, William, and the others, except for Wythe, must have been shocked by what they saw as they arrived at Richmond. The capital at that time was a rough assemblage of wooden buildings scattered along the shores of the James River. There were scarcely any brick buildings or grand avenues. They moved into a wooden frame house on top of Shockoe Hill—a house at the southeast corner of 5th and Grace Street, formerly owned by William Nelson. The small yellow house faced the river. Wythe could walk from his house to his Chancery Court chambers in the basement of the capitol. He took advantage of his free time to continue his studies of ancient Hebrew with local Rabbi Isaac Seixas, and he had a laboratory set up in his home where he and William Munford performed electrical experiments. For the next fifteen years, George Wythe would become a welcome and frequent visitor in the homes of Richmond dignitaries and would continue to instruct young men in his chambers or as private students in his home.

In 1800, Wythe represented Virginia in the Electoral College balloting for president. The vote in the Electoral College was tied, sending the decision to the House of Representatives. His good friend Thomas Jefferson emerged as the winner after lengthy balloting, defeating incumbent John Adams. Again in 1804, Wythe represented Virginia and cast his ballot for Jefferson in the Electoral College. This time Jefferson easily defeated challenger Charles Cotesworth Pinckney and won his second term.

During the last few years of his life, George Wythe had two young men in his household. One was a young former slave, Michael Brown, referred to as a mulatto. Wythe taught Michael to read and write and then began his education in Latin, Greek and science. Wythe's actions would have received condemnation by most of Richmond's residents. The second young man living with Wythe was his great-nephew, the grandson of Wythe's sister, Anne. George Wythe Sweeney shared his great-uncle's name, but not his character. He was a profligate teenager who spent his time gambling and carousing around Richmond. Perhaps George Wythe hoped to reform his great-nephew.

In 1803, Wythe made a will leaving bequests to Lydia, Michael, and another former slave. In this will, the bulk of Wythe's estate was left to George Wythe Sweeney. Three years later, Wythe wrote a codicil to his will directing that Michael be raised by Thomas Jefferson. Wythe provided that Jefferson would have access to his Bank of Virginia stock income to support and continue Michael's education. It is clear from this action that Wythe had great affection for Michael. He made no such guardianship provision for Sweeney.

By this time, Wythe was aware that Sweeney had been stealing from him. The boy had taken some of Wythe's books and, possibly, a terrestrial globe intended for Thomas Jefferson, and sold them on the street in Richmond. Wythe wrote a second codicil three weeks after the first. In that document he directed that his Bank of Virginia stock be divided with half going to Michael and the other half going to Sweeney.

One day, Lydia caught Sweeney going through Wythe's desk. Sweeney found blank checks in his great-uncle's desk; he also found Wythe's will and codicils. From those documents he learned that he would come into a sizeable estate when his great-uncle died; but that he would have to share it with a freed slave apparently was too much to bear for young Sweeney.

In April of 1806, he presented a check at the Bank of Virginia payable to himself and bearing a forged George Wythe signature. This forgery was soon followed by five or six more, and the bank manager turned the evidence over to the sheriff. On May 25th, George Wythe rose as usual, went to the well and drew a bucket of water, poured the water in the cistern of his shower, and then stood under the spout as the bracing cold water poured over him. He had performed this ritual for most of his eighty years. After dressing, he went into his study and began reading his paper. Lydia, attuned to the rhythm of her former master's day, began preparing his usual breakfast of eggs, toast and coffee.

As Lydia began frying the eggs, Sweeney entered the kitchen. She offered to cook breakfast for him. He said he would just have toast and coffee as he was in a hurry to go somewhere. While Lydia's back was turned, Sweeney poured himself a cup of coffee from the pot and apparently added a yellow powder to the pot. When Lydia turned, she saw Sweeney throw a scrap of paper into the fire.

Sweeney quickly ate his toast, drank his coffee, and left the house.

Lydia carried Wythe his breakfast, and then she and Michael had theirs in the kitchen as they usually did. Within a short time, Michael was gravely ill. He had excruciating abdominal cramps, nausea, and vomited repeatedly. Soon, Lydia experienced the same symptoms and, in her agony, discovered that George Wythe was similarly affected. Fortunately a doctor lived next door and he came immediately. But there was little he could do.

Perhaps because she had only taken a small sip of coffee, Lydia recovered and continued to care for Michael and Wythe. On his sick bed, Wythe examined checks delivered by a bank messenger and confirmed that they were forgeries. While Lydia attended to Wythe and Michael, the sheriff arrested George Wythe Sweeney on a charge of forgery and took him into custody. On June 1, Michael Brown died. An autopsy found signs of poisoning.

When Wythe heard of Michael's death he said, "I shall not be far behind." He called for his friend Edmund Randolph and dictated another codicil to his will. He clearly suspected that his great-nephew had poisoned him and murdered Michael. In the codicil he revoked all bequests to Sweeney and left his estate to Sweeney's siblings. After signing the codicil, he said, "It is not my desire that this unfortunate nephew of mine shall be prosecuted or punished, further than this codicil will punish him, for the offences which he stands charged. I dread such a stigma being cast upon my name or my sister's." The charge Wythe referred to at that time was forgery. Sweeney had not yet been charged with murder. Wythe, anticipating that his death was inevitable, requested that his body be autopsied as well. He also asked his friends to search Sweeney's room. They did so and discovered evidence of arsenic there.

On June 5th, Wythe said, "I am murdered." On Sunday, June 6th, he said, "Let me die righteous." Then he died.

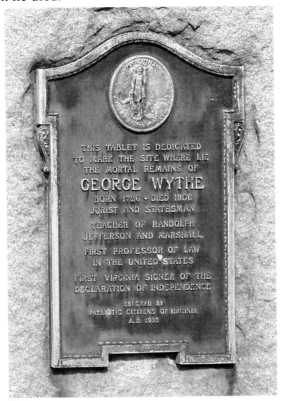

Memorial Tablet to George Wythe
at St. John's Churchyard, Richmond

George Wythe Sweeney eventually stood trial for the murder of his great-uncle. Lydia Broadnax could provide the most damning evidence. She had seen him reading Wythe's will, and she knew that no one else could have poisoned the coffee. She said, "I didn't see him, but it looks monstrous strange." Yellow arsenic powder was discovered in Sweeney's room and on his person. But the jury took only a few minutes to return a verdict of not guilty. The local newspaper, *The Enquirer*, reported that the strongest evidence, the testimony of the "negroes," was not admitted, thus leaving the prosecution with a weak case. The charges of forgery also failed to stick on appeal—Sweeney never stood trial for the murder of Michael Brown. Sweeney moved west, a free but impoverished man.

When news of George Wythe's death reached the citizens of Richmond, church bells rang throughout the city. He had been attended by an Anglican and a Presbyterian minister as he died. His body lay in state in the House of Delegates before burial at St. John's Church. *The Enquirer* issue of June 10, 1806 wrote: "Kings may require mausoleums to consecrate their memory, saints may claim the privilege of canonization; but the venerable George Wythe needs no other monument than the services rendered to his country, and the universal sorrow that country sheds over his grave."

George Wythe

Thus ended an eighty-year life of avid intellectual curiosity, decorum, and dedication to the highest principles of justice and service to others. George Wythe had greatly surpassed his ancestors in longevity, prosperity, and, most importantly, in public service. He had no children of his own, but he nurtured, guided and educated numerous young men, many of whom went on to distinguished public careers of their own, serving their country as President of the United States, U. S. Senator, and Chief Justice of the Supreme Court.

George Wythe's legacy also includes his mark on the constitution of the Commonwealth of Virginia and the U. S. Constitution. His name is bravely inscribed on the founding document of the new republic, *The Declaration of Independence,* testifying to his patriotism. As America's first law professor, George Wythe created the model for instruction still used in law schools today. He personally established a standard for the practice of law that has never been surpassed and seldom equaled in the last 250 years.

Acknowledgments

I want to thank the Williamsburg Writers for their review and editorial assistance with this biography in its rough stages.

Thanks also to Bob Hill, retail manager with the Colonial Williamsburg Foundation, for suggesting that I produce a short biography of George Wythe.

Image Credits

Cover illustration Portrait of George Wythe, image number 148-CD-13-9, courtesy of the U. S. National Archives and Records Administration.

P. 5 Reconstructed Capitol building, Williamsburg, photograph by author.

P. 9 Courthouse, Williamsburg, photograph by author.

P. 16 George Wythe House, Williamsburg, photograph by author.

P. 26 Wren Building, College of William and Mary, photograph by author.

P. 36 George Wythe Memorial, St. John's Churchyard, Richmond, photograph by author.